TRIO FOR Trumpets

22 Distinctive Arrangements of Famous Music

JOHN CACAVAS

CONTENTS

O Come, All Ye Faithful	2
The Yellow Rose of Texas	3
God Rest Ye Merry, Gentlemen	4
The Kerry Dance	5
Londonderry Air ("Danny Boy")	6
Grand March (from *Aida*)	7
Bugle Call Rag	8
Sweet Betsy from Pike	9
Deep River	10
Greensleeves	11
When Johnny Comes Marching Home	12
Joshua	13
America, the Beautiful	14
Red River Valley	15
The Great Gate of Kiev (from *Pictures at an Exhibition*)	16
Sarabande	17
Aura Lee	18
The Trumpet Tune	19
Pachelbel's Canon	20
When the Saints Go Marching In	22
Battle Hymn of the Republic	23
Fanfares	24

Copyright © MCMXCIV by Alfred Publishing Co., Inc.
All rights reserved.   Printed in USA.

Art Direction: Ted Engelbart
Cover Design: Martha Widmann
Photos: Courtesy of Yamaha Corporation of America

O Come, All Ye Faithful

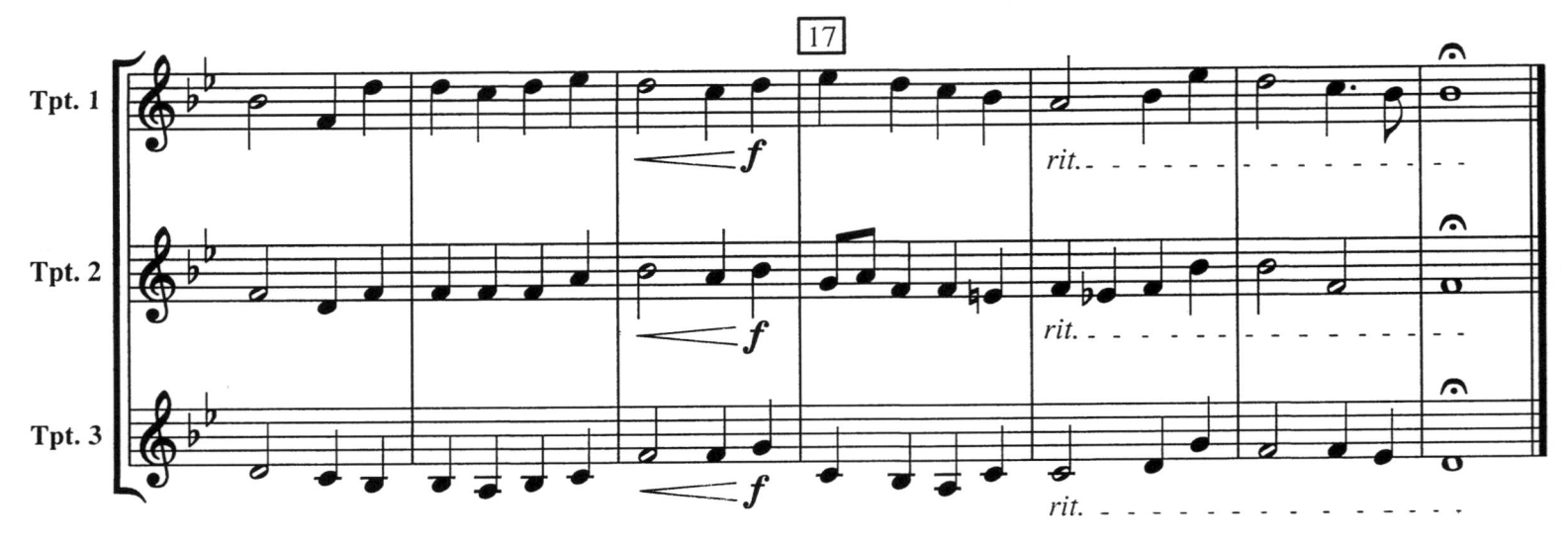

Wade
Arr. by John Cacavas

The Yellow Rose of Texas

J. K.
Arr. by John Cacavas

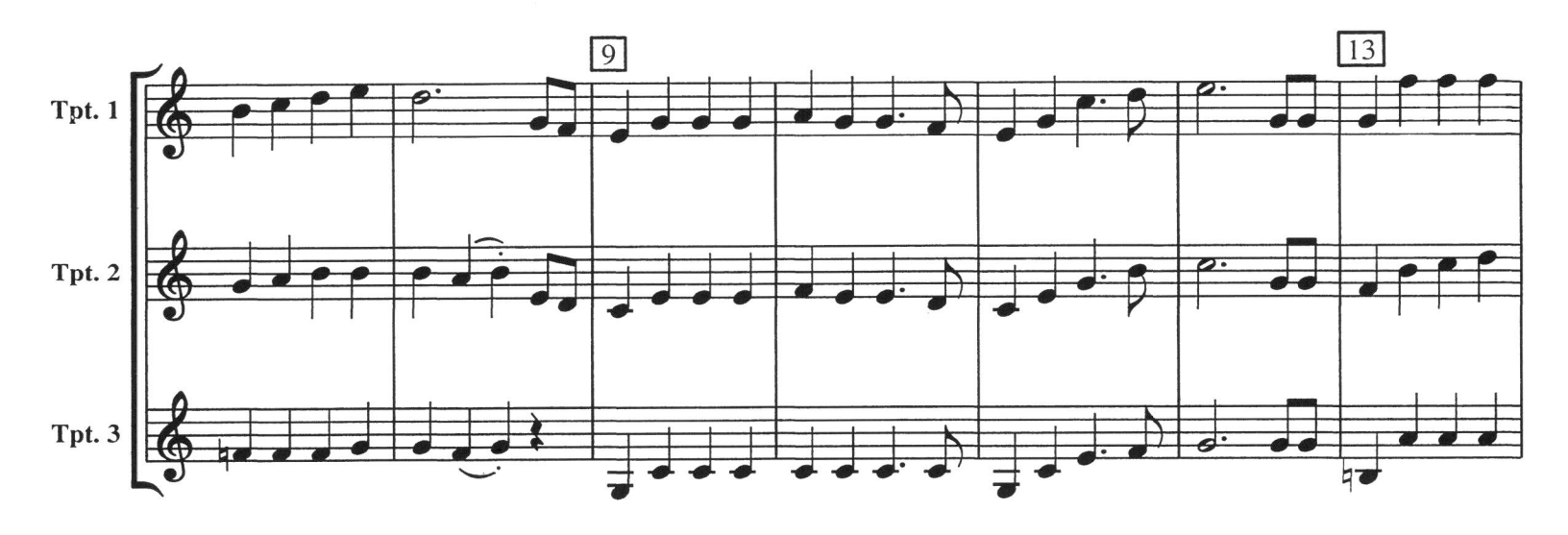

God Rest Ye Merry, Gentlemen

Traditional English Carol
Arr. by John Cacavas

The Kerry Dance

Irish Folk Song
Arr. by John Cacavas

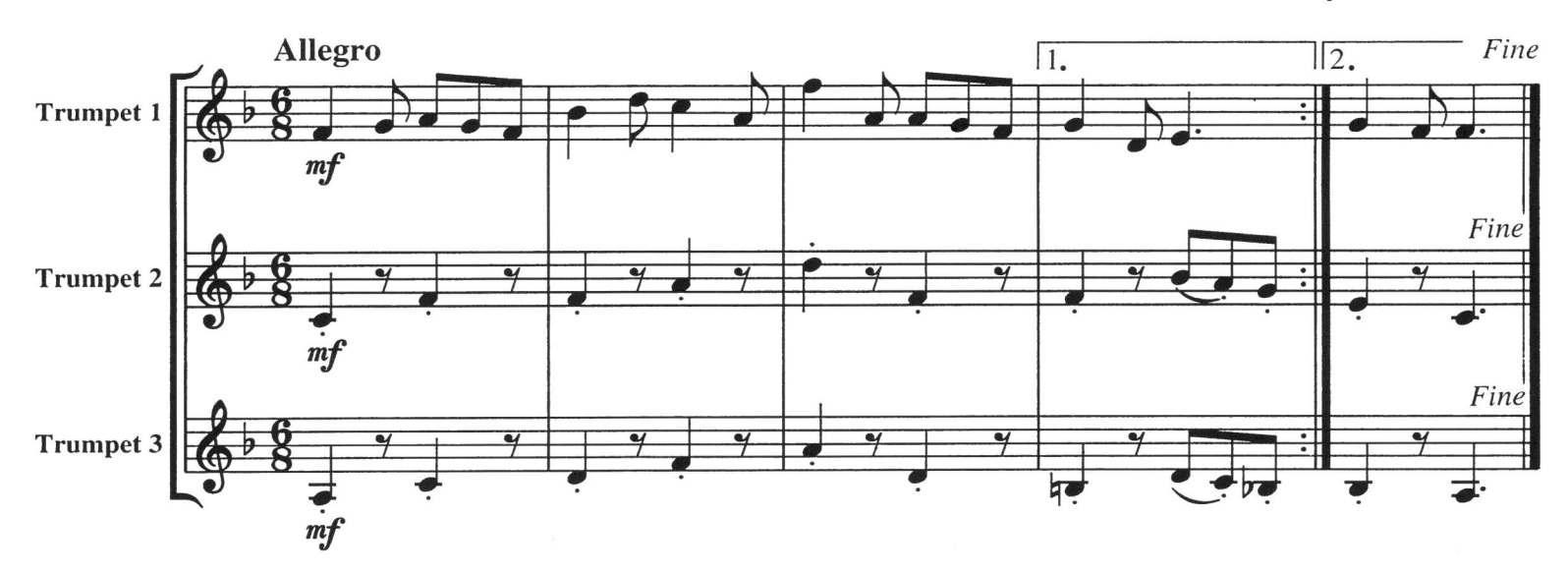

Londonderry Air
("Danny Boy")

Traditional Irish Folk Song
Arr. by John Cacavas

Grand March

(from *Aida*)

Verdi
Arr. by John Cacavas

Bugle Call Rag

John Cacavas

Sweet Betsy from Pike

Traditional Folk Song
Arr. by John Cacavas

Deep River

Traditional Spiritual
Arr. by John Cacavas

Greensleeves

Traditional
Arr. by John Cacavas

When Johnny Comes Marching Home

Gilmore
Arr. by John Cacavas

Joshua

Traditional Spiritual
Arr. by John Cacavas

America, the Beautiful

Ward
Arr. by John Cacavas

Red River Valley

Traditional Folk Song
Arr. by John Cacavas

The Great Gate of Kiev

(from *Pictures at an Exhibition*)

Mussorgsky
Arr. by John Cacavas

Sarabande

Couperin
Arr. by John Cacavas

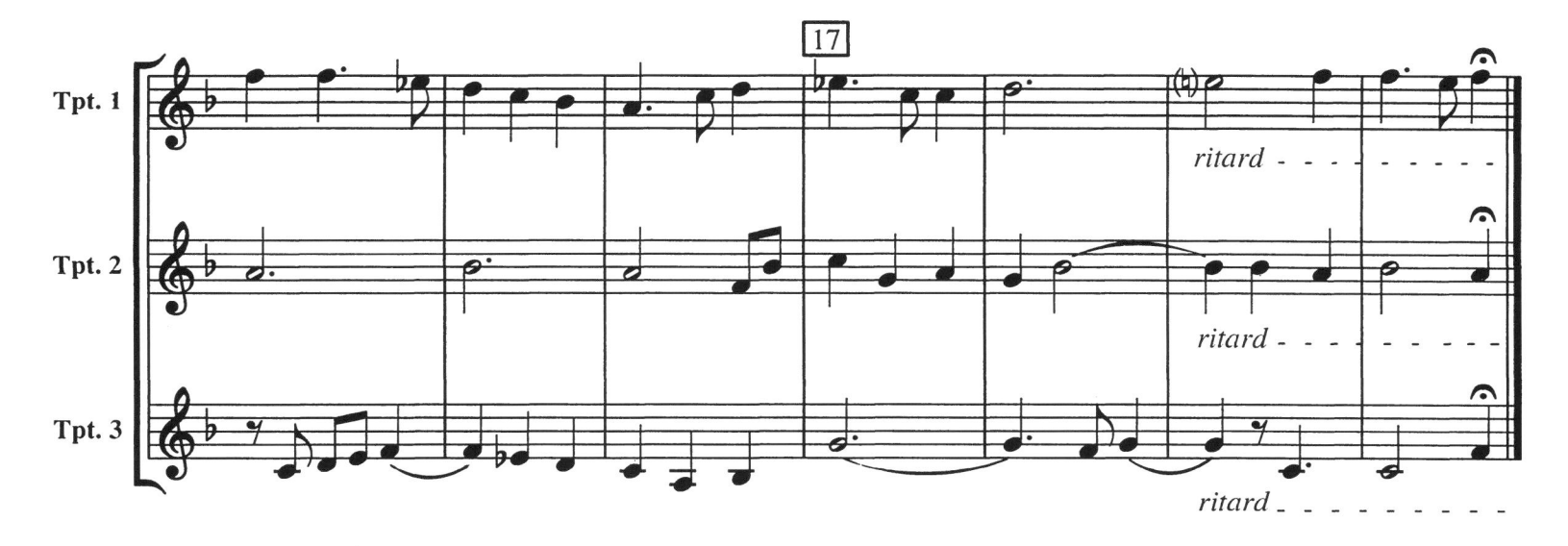

Aura Lee

Poulton
Arr. by John Cacavas

The Trumpet Tune

Purcell
Arr. by John Cacavas

Pachelbel's Canon

Pachelbel
Arr. by John Cacavas

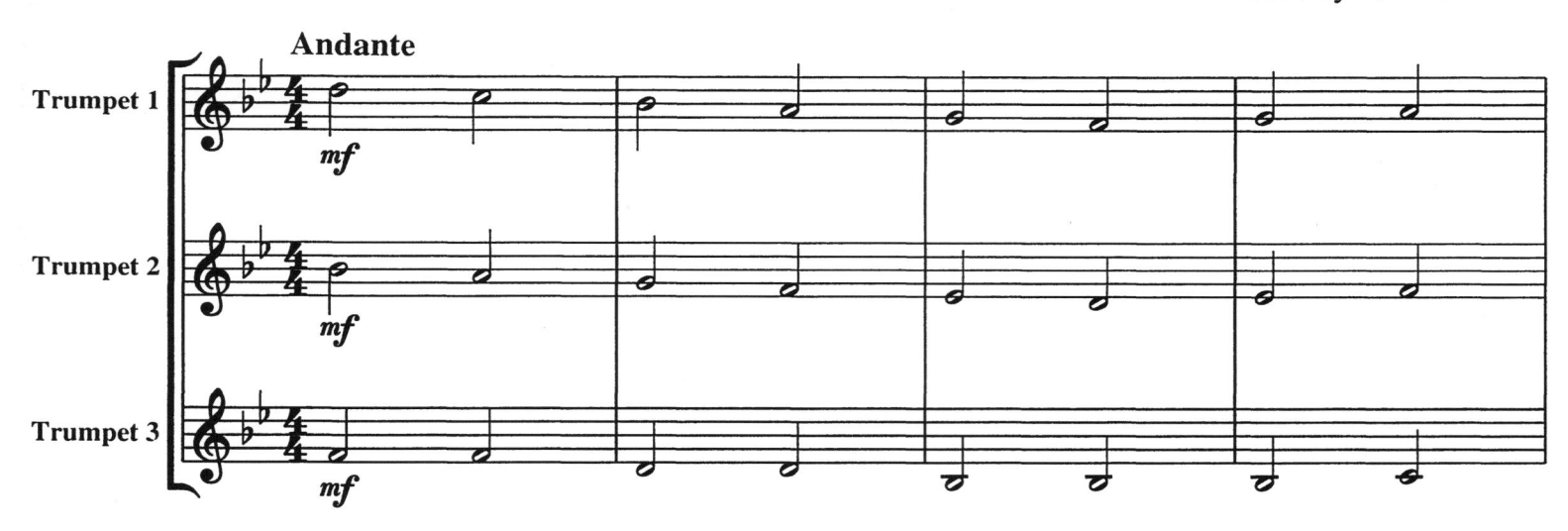

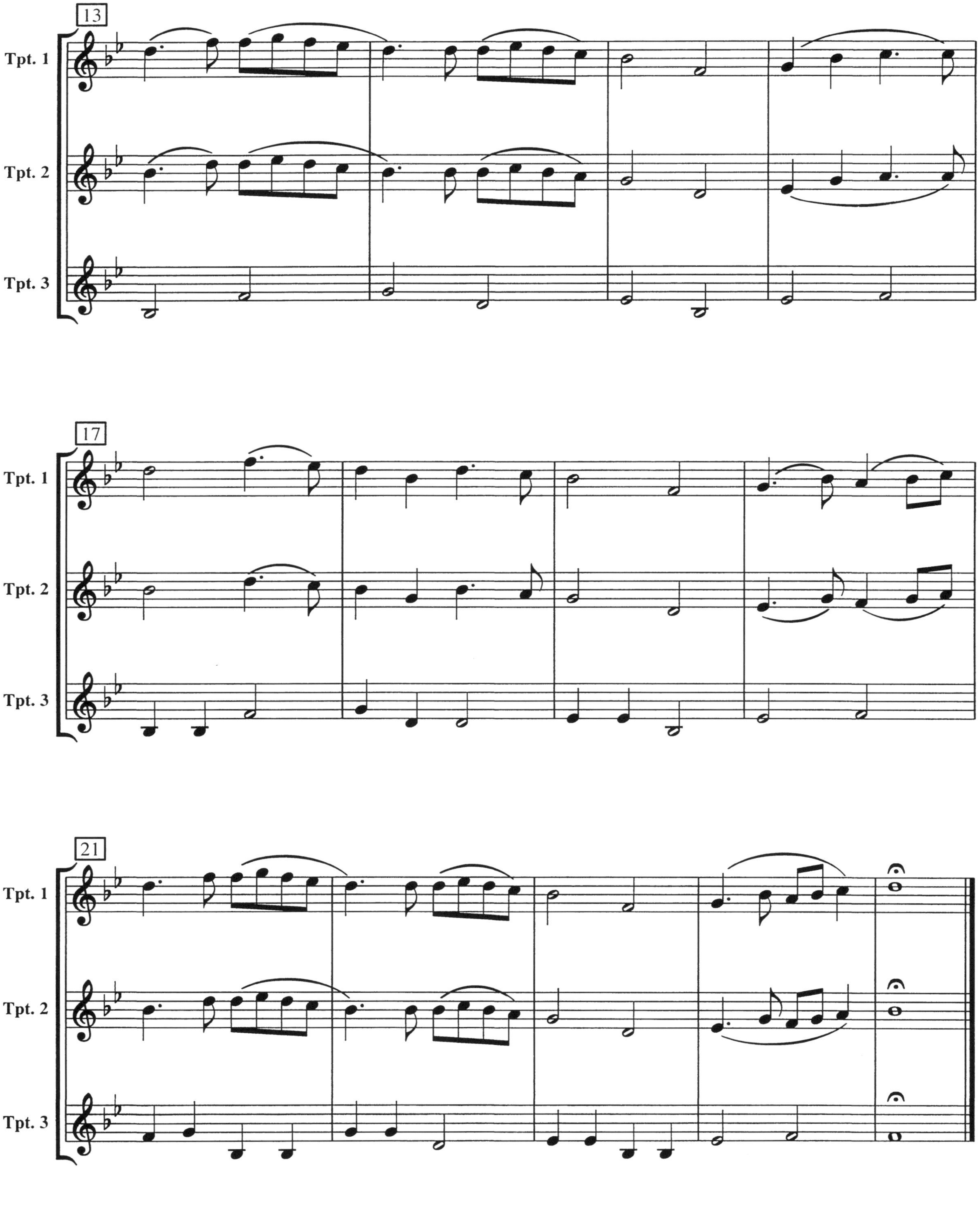
13
Tpt. 1
Tpt. 2
Tpt. 3
17
Tpt. 1
Tpt. 2
Tpt. 3
21
Tpt. 1
Tpt. 2
Tpt. 3

When the Saints Go Marching In

Black
Arr. by John Cacavas

Battle Hymn of the Republic

Howe
Arr. by John Cacavas

Fanfares

John Cacavas